KU-479-011

LITTLE BOOK
OF
BIG IDEAS

www.**books**at**trans**world.co.uk

LITTLE BOOK
OF
BIG IDEAS

THE EDEN PROJECT TEAM

With cartoons by Alan Clarke

eden project books

LIFE ON EARTH has survived volcanic eruptions worse than any nuclear war, and a complete change of atmosphere from one with huge amounts of carbon dioxide to one with huge amounts of oxygen. But if ⇨

⇨ the loss of biodiversity through human impact goes too far, humans themselves will be among its first victims.

Think of a pilot who notices that the rivets on the wings of his plane are falling out one by one. It is impossible for him to judge how long he has left before the plane falls apart – but he knows that if he is going to survive he must do something, and quickly.

'We're not running out of resources – we're just turning them into rubbish we can't use again.'

*Edwin Datschefski,
environmentalist*

IF EVERYBODY IN THE UK switched off their telly at night instead of leaving it on standby, we could save £50m a year in energy costs. Then there's the video, the DVD player,

the hi-fi . . . just think, no
more annoying red lights in
the darkness!

www.esru.strath.ac.uk

'The greatest service which
can be rendered any country
is to add a useful plant to its
culture.'

*Thomas Jefferson, third President of
the United States, 1800*

THE AMAZONIAN 'DIESEL TREE' (*Copaifera langsdorfii*) can produce 220 litres of sap a day. The sap is so similar to diesel fuel that it can be used in truck engines.

www.hort.purdue.edu

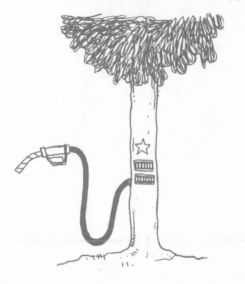

HEMP HAS OVER 25,000 legal uses and only one illegal use, yet you still need a licence to grow it in the UK. One acre of hemp can produce as much usable fibre as four acres of trees and two acres of cotton. Hemp is certainly a growth industry: in 1993 the worldwide value of hemp products was $US5m, rising to over $US150m by 2000.

www.naihc.org

'This "telephone" has too
many shortcomings to be
seriously considered as a
means of communication.
The device is inherently of
no value to us.'

Western Union
internal memo, 1876

UNTIL 1883 UP TO 90 per cent of all paper was made with hemp fibre – the Gutenberg Bible, the Declaration of Independence and the US Constitution were all first printed on hemp paper. It is stronger than paper made from wood pulp and can be recycled up to seven times compared with wood pulp's four – and is acid- and chlorine-free.

www.naihc.org

BOTTLED WATER COSTS TWICE
as much as petrol, three
times as much as milk –
and ten thousand times as
much as tap water! Then
there's the 1.5 million
tonnes of plastic that goes
into making the bottles
every year.

Whatever some drinks
companies would have you

believe, tap water is
perfectly safe to drink – and
you've already paid for it.

www.greennature.com

'Until man duplicates a blade of grass, nature can laugh at his so-called scientific knowledge . . . It's obvious that we don't know one millionth of one per cent about anything.'

Thomas Alva Edison

SUGAR IS UNDER ATTACK as a food additive, but the 'baggasse', the residue of the cane once the sugar has been extracted, can be used as a source of fuel for producing electricity. In Hawaii this product has become the major income generator, and it is the sugar that is the by-product

– in fact, some forms of *Saccharum robustum* have been produced that contain no sugar at all!

OVER THREE-QUARTERS OF ALL
natural rubber goes into
making tyres – 860 million
in 1990. In the UK over 40
million tyres were replaced
in 1999; until recently they
would all have gone into
landfill, but now over 70
per cent of them are
recycled and reused to
make anything from
dustbins to car parts.

30

'What is the good of having a
nice house without a decent
planet to put it on?'

Henry David Thoreau

CONVENTIONAL DESALINATION uses large amounts of energy, usually derived from fossil fuels. Seawater greenhouses provide fresh water for agriculture in arid coastal regions, using cheap and simple technology.

This process uses seawater to cool and ventilate a large greenhouse, and sun to distil fresh water from seawater. Successful tests have been carried out on Tenerife and in Abu Dhabi.

www.seawatergreenhouse.com

DOES THE MILKMAN STILL deliver in your area? Make sure he continues to do so by having your milk delivered. Milk bottles are used up to twenty times before being recycled, unlike plastic bottles and cartons.

www.wasteonline.org.uk

'A plant is like a self-willed man, out of whom we can obtain all which we desire, if we will only treat him his own way.'

Goethe

SUSTRANS – THE UK's sustainable transport charity – will have created 10,000 miles of cycle routes throughout the UK by 2005, including a growing network of safe cycle routes to schools. The St Austell

branch of the Cornish Way
route runs through the
Eden Project. Why not cycle
to Eden next time – and get
in cheaper?

www.sustrans.org

FLYING A KILO OF APPLES to Britain from New Zealand in the spring will produce a kilo of CO_2; a kilo of well-stored English apples bought locally produces only 50mg.

Paul Waddington, **Seasonal Food**

WISE WORDS WISE WORDS WISE WORDS WISE WORDS

'And we should consider every day lost on which we have not danced at least once. And we should call every truth false which was not accompanied by at least one laugh.'

Friedrich Wilhelm Nietzsche

WHAT HAS MAIZE DONE for us?
Just a few things . . .
popcorn, cornflour, whisky,
canned food, shoe polish,
fireworks, crayons, inks,
marshmallows, mustard,
ice cream, cosmetics,
plastics, acetone, industrial
alcohol . . . an industrial

feedstock, ethanol, glycerol, citric and lactic acids . . . corn syrup in puddings, sweets, toothpaste and cakes . . . cornmeal in soaps, corn oil in foods, paints, polishes and varnishes . . . starch on sheets and shirts, grain ⇨

46

⇨ for poultry and beef, stems for silage, leaves for cigarettes and mats, spent cobs for fuel . . . and that's before anybody thought of genetically modifying it!

www.maize.agron.iastate.edu

VOLATILE ORGANIC COMPOUNDS (VOCs) associated with petrochemical-based paint thinners can be harmful to painters exposed to them for long periods. Calendula oil obtained from pot marigold seeds does the same job – without the damaging side-effects.

www.nf_2000.org

'A weed is a plant that has mastered every survival skill except for learning how to grow in rows.'

Doug Larson,
American cartoonist

KEEPING A CHILD IN disposable nappies costs at least £1000 a year. Using cloth nappies saves around £600 a year for the first child, and £800 for the second if the same nappies are used, even including the energy costs of washing them.

www.greenparty.org.uk

BIOMASS – USED RENEWABLE plant material as fuel, as opposed to irreplaceable plant-based fossil fuels – is underestimated or taken for granted. Elephant grass (*Miscanthus sinensis*) is under investigation as a good source of biomass. It regrows annually when cut, and tall bundles of dried grass are burned in large boilers to create energy, mainly in schools and hospitals. It can be grown on underused agricultural or urban fringe land, and makes an attractive environment for birds.

www.pgen.com

'Computers in
the future may
weigh no more than 1.5 tons.'

Popular Mechanics,
*forecasting the relentless march of
science, 1949*

ONLY 2.5 PER CENT OF WORLD mango production reaches the supermarket shelves – the rest are consumed where they are grown in over 85 countries, sometimes as famine food.

One fruit pretty much provides an adult's daily vitamin C requirement. The kernel provides oil for beauty creams and can even provide protein. The trees can continue fruiting ⇨

⇨ for hundreds of years, but dead wood can be used in house construction and furniture making, the bark in tanning (and gum from the bark is used to mend crockery!).

www.mad4mango.com

RADICAL GLOBAL WARMING
solutions include capturing
CO_2 and storing it out of
harm's way, or allowing CO_2
to accumulate so it deflects
heat from the sun back into
space. Mega-engineering
projects to reflect the sun's ⇨

⇨ rays include giant mirrors, reflective aluminium balloons – and giant whisks in the ocean, throwing salt spray into the atmosphere to whiten clouds! CO_2 can be stored by seeding the southern oceans with iron

to encourage plankton
bloom, or by burying CO_2
from factory emissions
in the ground (geological
storage) or in aquifers deep
in the ocean floor.

New Scientist *February 2004*

WISE WORDS WISE WORDS WISE WORDS WISE WORDS WISE WORDS

'Play is the beginning of knowledge.'

George A. Dorsey, American anthropologist (1868–1931)

GOT A HEALTH PROBLEM?
Try plants:

GRAPES for diseased gums
and skin complaints

LIMES for colds

BLACKBERRIES for eye and
mouth infections

PINEAPPLES for indigestion

PASSION FRUIT has a
tranquillizing effect on
your body. Eat them before
you go to sleep and you will
dream sweet dreams

TEA MAY NEUTRALIZE carcinogens. Tests on survivors of the atomic bombing of Hiroshima and Nagasaki indicated a significantly lower level in the incidence of cancer in heavy tea drinkers compared to those who did not drink tea.

Cancer Causes and Control 12, 2001

'The true meaning of life is
to plant trees, under whose
shade you do not expect
to sit.'

Nelson Henderson

EACH ONE-DEGREE CHANGE you make to your central heating thermostat – down in summer, up in winter – can save you up to 10 per cent on your heating bill, as well as cutting down on greenhouse gas emissions.

www.care2.com

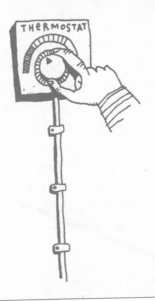

CASHEW NUT SHELL LIQUID (CNSL) sits in pockets within the cashew shell and contains anacardic acid, which prevents the ripening nuts from being eaten by monkeys – and causes blisters in humans unwise enough to eat them without roasting them first!

An oil extracted from CNSL has a much more benign use, however – it forms the heat-absorbing resin component of car brake shoes.

www.originalnuthouse.com

'The real miracle is not
walking on water or in thin air,
but to walk on earth.'

Thich Nhat Hanh (1926–),
Vietnamese Buddhist monk, poet
and peace activist.

WE USE ABOUT 8 BILLION non-biodegradable plastic bags a year in the UK, weighing about 10,000 tonnes. Every one of them goes into a landfill site – if it doesn't end up stuck in a tree, that is. But help is at hand. Perfectly adequate bags can be made from biodegradable plant-based plastics. Starch (typically ⇨

⇨ from maize, wheat and potatoes) or fermented plant sugars can produce Polylactic Acid (PLA) – a starting-point for the manufacture of plastics. A UK firm is already making food trays from starch derived from surplus potatoes.

www.environmentawards.net

THE CONSTRUCTION INDUSTRY is highly energy-inefficient, producing a disproportionate amount of waste and using non-biodegradable materials. Plant-based materials can reduce the environmental impact of construction – and at the ⇨

⇨ same time provide
alternative crops for
farmers to grow in a climate
of dwindling agriculture.
Natural fibres in the form
of insulation materials
and board products are
effective and allow
easy disposal through
composting; paints made

from natural materials produce little or no air pollutants; timber from rapidly renewable sources protects natural forests; recycled aggregates reduce waste.

www.natural-building.co.uk

'The earth laughs in flowers.'

Ralph Waldo Emerson

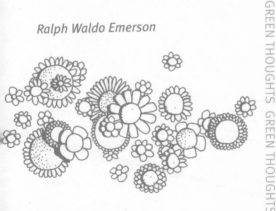

ONLY 5 PER CENT OF THE
world's plant species
have had the full
spectrum of their
pharmaceutical potential
tested in laboratories.
The contributions of willow
(aspirin), opium poppies
(heroin, codeine,
morphine) and cinchona
(quinine) to our health (or
otherwise) are well known,
but it is only in recent

years that high-profile treatments for cancer have been extracted from the rosy periwinkle and Pacific yew.

www.rain-tree.com

THE ENERGY PRODUCED BY
the recycling of one glass
bottle can power your TV
for a whole evening.

www.actionenergy.org.uk

'In the end we will conserve only what we love. We will love only what we understand. We will understand only what we are taught.'

Attributed to Baba Dioum, Senegalese conservationist

WHEN CONSUMERS BUY FAIRLY traded goods, they support communities in developing countries, cutting out the middleman and directing money back to those who need it most. Buying local produce supports local farmers and reduces food miles; buying organic food helps to take pesticides out of the food chain; buying recycled products minimizes the use of further resources.

Harnessing your buying power is a large step towards taking responsibility for your social and natural environment.

Your wallet is your weapon!

www.fairtrade.org.uk

'I have travelled the length
and breadth of this country
and talked with the best
people, and I can assure you
that data processing is a fad
that won't last out the year.'

*Editor in charge of business books
for Prentice Hall, 1957*

THE WORLD AVERAGE GRAIN production in 1998-9 was 356kg per person, a figure that reflects extremes of 1,156kg in North America and 146kg in sub-Saharan Africa. There is more than enough food in the world to feed it, yet 40 million people die of hunger each year while huge amounts of grain and pulses are fed to animals, lost to pests, rotted between harvest and consumption or destroyed to protect market values.

Erik Millstone and Tim Lang, **The Atlas of Food**

98

'Coming here today, I have no hidden agenda. I am fighting for my future . . . At school you teach us to behave in the world. You teach us not to fight with others, to work things out, to respect others, to clean up our mess, not ⇨

⇨ to hurt other creatures, to share and not be greedy. Then why do you go out and do those things you teach us not to do?'

Severn Cullis-Suzuki (12) addressing the Rio Earth Summit, June 1992

SWITCHING OFF NON-ESSENTIAL office equipment for one night can save enough energy to power a small car for a hundred miles.

**ActionEnergy /
www.actionenergy.org.uk**

IN SEVENTEENTH-CENTURY
London, a pocketful of
nutmeg was worth a
mansion in Holborn,
and only workers with
no pockets were allowed
to unload the ships. On
the Banda Islands in the
Moluccas, the only place in
the world where the plant
grew, ten pounds of nutmeg

cost a penny;
the cost in
London was
6,000 times
as much.

Giles Milton,
**Nathaniel's
Nutmeg**

FANCY A FAG? THE US Environmental Protection Agency lists 450 pesticides cleared for use on tobacco. They include Aldicarb, less than one-thousandth of an ounce of which is lethal for humans; Chlorpyriphos, linked to birth defects and damage to the male reproductive system; and

Telone, which causes kidney damage and respiratory problems.

SCIENTISTS COMPARED THE production costs of glass-reinforced plastic (GRP) panels for an Audi A3 with those for a biocomposite panel made from hemp or flax. Life-cycle analysis – the study of physical and environmental costs of a product from 'cradle to grave' – favoured the biocomposite panel. A major contributory factor was the cost of fuel saved over the life of the car because of the lower weight of biocomposites.

www.hemp.co.uk

'The best friend on earth of man is the tree: when we use the tree respectfully and economically we have one of the greatest resources of the earth.'

Frank Lloyd Wright,
American architect

BAMBOO IS THE MOST VIGOROUS woody plant on the planet – growing up to 1m a day in some cases, one-third faster than the fastest tree. It is also one of the strongest – almost 20 per cent stronger than steel. In Limon, Costa Rica, only the bamboo houses remained standing after a violent earthquake in 1992. It would take only five years and a plot of land 20m² to grow enough bamboo to build two 8m x 8m houses.

Bamboo is the fastest-growing way of regreening degraded areas and generates more oxygen than the equivalent area of trees.

www.worldbamboocongress.com

IN BRITAIN EACH OF US THROWS away twenty times our own bodyweight in rubbish every year. Nationally, that's enough to fill the Albert Hall twenty-four times a day. But we're running out of holes in the ground to fill up with our rubbish:

REDUCE, REUSE, RECYCLE!

www.defra.gov.uk

'Where is the life we have lost
in living?
Where is the wisdom we have
lost in knowledge?
Where is the knowledge we
have lost in information?'

T. S. Eliot, The Chorus of the Rock

IF WE ALL BOILED ONLY THE amount of water we needed, rather than a kettleful, we could save enough energy to power every street lamp in the UK for a night.

**ActionEnergy /
www.actionenergy.org.uk**

PLANTS CAN BRING PEOPLE
together; gardening is
therapeutic. Transforming
Violence's projects include
Jail Garden, where inmates
grow food for AIDS projects
and homeless shelters;
Rabbis for Human Rights,
a group of over a hundred
rabbis from every
denomination of Judaism
who participate in
replanting olive groves

destroyed by the Israeli
army in Palestine; and the
Medical Foundation for the
Care of Victims of Torture,
where garden programmes
help to bridge some of
the cultural and language
barriers that exist between
survivors of torture and
those helping the healing
process.

**www.transformingviolence.org–click on
'gardens'**

'. . . and the day came when the risk to remain tight in a bud was more painful than the risk it took to blossom.'

Anaïs Nin

ALSO FROM EDEN PROJECT BOOKS:

ADULT TITLES

Eden
Tim Smit

The complete story, from conception to completion, of the astounding Eden Project, illustrated with 32 pages of striking colour photographs.

0 552 14920 9; Pb non-fiction – £7.99

Plants for People
Anna Lewington

This pioneering book provides a fascinating insight into the ways in which we use plants – from woodpulp in our clothing to the sunflower and rape seeds providing cleaner fuel for our cars.

1 903 91908 8; Hb non-fiction – £20.00

An Ear to the Ground
Ken Thompson

What's really going on in your garden? This entertaining book shows how a little botanical knowledge can bring not just better results but peace of mind.

1 903 91919 3; Hb non-fiction – £10.00

The Architecture of Eden
Hugh Pearman and Andrew Whalley

Beautifully designed and illustrated, this is the inside story of how one of the architectural wonders of the world was designed and constructed.

1 903 91915 0; Hb non-fiction – £35.00

The Origin of Plants
Maggie Campbell-Culver

This critically acclaimed book tells the fascinating story of how and why Britain's spectacular gardens and private and public collections are home to the widest range of plants of any nation on earth.

1 903 91940 1; Pb non-fiction – £9.99

Seasonal Food
Paul Waddington

A month-by-month guide to British produce in season, with regional information and supplier advice. Indispensable for anyone who cares about good food, the environment and the relationship between the two.

1 903 91952 5; Tpb non-fiction – £10.99

CHILDREN'S TITLES

The World Came to My Place Today
Jo Readman and Ley Honor Roberts

An entertaining and thought-provoking bedtime story that explains how plants from all over the world affect children's lives.

1 903 91902 9; Pb non-fiction – £5.99

A Child's Guide to Wild Flowers
Charlotte Voake

A visually stunning and indispensable guide to the wild flowers that you see every day; by the road, as garden weeds, or between the cracks in the pavement – as well as on trips to the country or seaside.

1 903 91910 X; Hb non-fiction – £10.99

Adam and Eve and the Garden of Eden
Jane Ray

A beautiful and vibrant retelling of the story of the Garden of Eden – it remains faithful to the biblical text, whilst acknowledging the many creation stories told all over the world.

1 903 91906 1; Hb fiction – £10.99

My Flower, Your Flower
Melanie Walsh

A fun and colourful look at the differences and similarities between plants for the very young.

1 903 91928 2; Pb fiction – £5.99

TRANSWORLD PUBLISHERS
61-63 Uxbridge Road, London W5 5SA
a division of The Random House Group Ltd

RANDOM HOUSE AUSTRALIA (PTY) LTD
20 Alfred Street, Milsons Point, Sydney,
New South Wales 2061, Australia

RANDOM HOUSE NEW ZEALAND LTD
18 Poland Road, Glenfield, Auckland 10, New Zealand

RANDOM HOUSE SOUTH AFRICA (PTY) LTD
Endulini, 5a Jubilee Road, Parktown 2193, South Africa

Published 2004 by Eden Project Books
a division of Transworld Publishers

Copyright © the Eden Project Ltd 2004
Cartoons © Alan Clarke 2004

The publishers have made every reasonable effort to contact
the copyright owners of the quotations reproduced in this
book. In the few cases where they have been unsuccessful
they invite copyright holders to contact them direct.

The right of the Eden Project Ltd to be identified as the
author of this work has been asserted in accordance with
sections 77 and 78 of the Copyright, Designs and Patents
Act 1988.

A catalogue record for this book is available from the
British Library.
ISBN 1903 919517

All rights reserved. No part of this publication may be
reproduced, stored in a retrieval system, or transmitted in any
form or by any means, electronic, mechanical, photocopying,
recording, or otherwise, without the prior permission of the
publishers.

Typeset in 14/17 pt Novarese
by Falcon Oast Graphic Art Ltd.

Printed in
Italy

1 3 5 7 9 10 8 6 4 2

Papers used by Eden Project Books are natural, recyclable
products made from wood grown in sustainable forests. The
manufacturing processes conform to the environmental
regulations of the country of origin.